CONTENTS

NOTE

By using open strings, all the pieces in this album, except *Innocence* (Haydn), may be played in the first position. Some small liberties have been taken in one or two of the melodies so that unduly awkward technical problems might be avoided.

W.F.

EASY CLASSICS FOR THE CELLO

Book 1

Arranged by
WATSON FORBES

1. CHORAL

Harmonised by
J. S. BACH (1685-1750)

Extra cello parts are on sale

Easy Classics for the Cello

2. A DISTANT LAND (Op. 15, No. 1.)

(In der Fremde)

from 'Scenes of Childhood'

R. SCHUMANN (1810-56)

3. MINUET IN G

H. PURCELL (1659-95)

4. AN OLD FRENCH SONG (Op. 39, No. 16)

from 'Album for the Young'

P. TCHAIKOWSKY (1840-93)

5. THE BLACKSMITH (Op. 19, No. 4)

(Der Schmied)

J. BRAHMS (1833-97)

Allegro (♩ = 168)

6. MARCH

from 'Flavius'

G. F. HANDEL (1685-1759)

EASY CLASSICS FOR THE CELLO

Book 1

Arranged by

WATSON FORBES

CELLO

1. CHORAL

Harmonised by
J. S. BACH (1685-1750)

2. A DISTANT LAND (Op. 15, No. 1.)

(In der Fremde)

from 'Scenes of Childhood'

R. SCHUMANN (1810-56)

3. MINUET IN G

H. PURCELL (1659-95)

4. AN OLD FRENCH SONG (Op. 39, No. 16)
from 'Album for the Young'

P. TCHAIKOWSKY (1840-93)

5. THE BLACKSMITH (Op. 19, No. 4)
(Der Schmied)

J. BRAHMS (1833-97)

6. MARCH
from 'Flavius'

G. F. HANDEL (1685-1759)

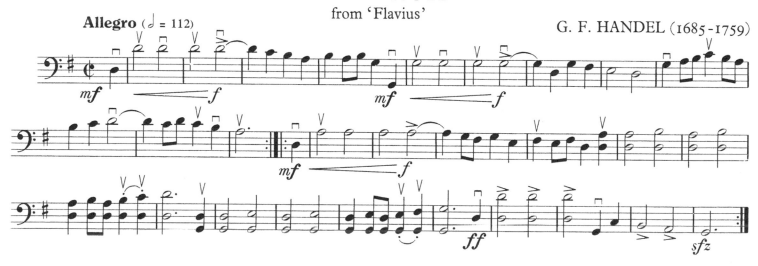

7. A TRIFLE
(Le Petit-rien)

F. COUPERIN (1668-1733)

Easy Classics for the Cello

continued on next page

8. INNOCENCE
from Op. 53, No. 1

J. HAYDN (1732-1809)

9. CHACONNE

G. F. HANDEL (1685-1759)

10. THE MERRY PEASANT (Op. 68, No. 10)
from 'Album for the Young'

R. SCHUMANN (1810-56)

Easy Classics for the Cello

11. WIEGENLIED (Lullaby)

W. A. MOZART-BERNHARD FLIES *

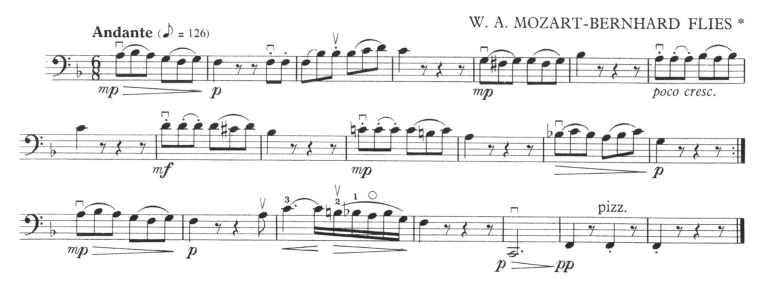

12. SERENADE
(An den Mond)

F. SCHUBERT (1797-1828)

13. ECOSSAISE

L. van BEETHOVEN (1770-1827)

* Well known as a song by Mozart, this Wiegenlied is now known to be the composition of Bernhard Flies

Processed and printed by
Halstan & Co. Ltd., Amersham, Bucks., England

OXFORD UNIVERSITY PRESS

7. A TRIFLE

(Le Petit-rien)

F. COUPERIN (1668-1733)

8. INNOCENCE
from Op. 53, No. 1

J. HAYDN (1732-1809)

Easy Classics for the Cello

9. CHACONNE

G. F. HANDEL (1685-1759)

10. THE MERRY PEASANT (Op. 68, No. 10)
from 'Album for the Young'

R. SCHUMANN (1810-56)

Easy Classics for the Cello

11. WIEGENLIED (Lullaby)

W. A. MOZART-BERNHARD FLIES *

* Well known as a song by Mozart, this Wiegenlied is now known to be the composition of Bernhard Flies

Easy Classics for the Cello

12. SERENADE
(An den Mond)

F. SCHUBERT (1797-1828)

Easy Classics for the Cello

13. ECOSSAISE

L. van BEETHOVEN (1770-1827)

Processed and printed by
Halstan & Co. Ltd., Amersham, Bucks., England

OXFORD UNIVERSITY PRESS